ALL ABOUT ANIMALS IN THE SNOW

All About Snowy Owls

Kerrily Sapet

EZ READERS
AN IMPRINT OF MITCHELL LANE PUBLISHERS

CREATING YOUNG NONFICTION READERS

EZ Readers offer nonfiction for beginning readers in PreK through first grade, using simple language, clear illustrations, and engaging facts to build vocabulary and confidence.

TIPS FOR READING NONFICTION WITH BEGINNING READERS

Talk about Nonfiction

Begin by explaining that nonfiction books give us information that is true. The book will be organized around a specific topic or idea, and we may learn new facts through reading.

Look at the Parts

Most nonfiction books have helpful features. Our *EZ Readers* include color photographs and graphic aids, a table of contents, a glossary, and an index. Share the purpose of these features with your reader.

Color Photos and Graphic Aids

A lot of information can be found by "reading" photos, charts, maps, and other graphic aids found within nonfiction texts. Help your reader learn more about the different ways information can be displayed.

Table of Contents

Located at the front of the book, this list shows the big ideas within the text and the page numbers where they can be found.

Glossary

Located at the back of the book, the glossary defines key words and phrases that are related to the topic. These words and phrases can be found in the text in colored type.

Index

Located at the back of the book, an index is an alphabetical list of topics and the page numbers where they can be found.

With a little help and guidance about reading nonfiction, you can feel good about introducing a young reader to the world of *EZ Readers* nonfiction books.

EZ Readers is an imprint of:

Mitchell Lane
PUBLISHERS

2001 SW 31st Avenue
Hallandale, FL 33009
mitchelllanepub.com

First Edition, 2026.

Author: Kerrily Sapet
Editor: Morgan Brody

ISBN 979-8-89260-852-7 (library binding)
ISBN 979-8-90145-045-1 (paperback)
ISBN 979-8-89260-949-4 (ebook)

LC record available at https://lccn.loc.gov/2025950872

Photo credits: Adobe, Pixasquare, cover, 1, 2, 3, 4, 8, 11, 15,19, 21, 22, 23, 24; Adobe, Tukinoto, cover, 1; Shutterstock, FotoRequest, cover, 1; Adobe, Alpha Vector, 3, 9, 12, 14, 18, 22; Shutterstock, ggala, 5; Shutterstock, Jim Cumming, 6–7; Shutterstock, Piotr Krzeslak, 9; Shutterstock, Naoto Shinkai, 9; Shutterstock, Holger Kirk, 10, 22; Shutterstock, Wang LiQiang, 12–13; Shutterstock, vicspacewalker, 14; Shutterstock, Liakhomtsev, 18, 22; Shutterstock, LouieLea, 20, 22; Shutterstock, clarst5, 21; Shutterstock, grayjay, 22; Shutterstock, Alones, 22; Shutterstock, Angelica Sunmark, 22

Table of Contents

Meeting An Arctic Animal

Imagine walking outside in the winter. Snow crunches under your boots. The wind is cold. Your coat keeps you warm.

You look up and see a bird flying. It's white like the snow. A snowy owl! Each wing is as wide as a door. Snowy owls are as tall as big dogs and as heavy as small cats. They live in the **Arctic**—one of the coldest places on Earth.

Snowy Owl Watching

You can see the snowy owl's round head and yellow eyes. It has thick, warm feathers. The owl's feet are also covered with feathers, like it's wearing slippers.

OUTSTANDING OWLS!

Male snowy owls are white. Females are white with brown stripes.

You hear a loud “hoo, hooo.” Snowy owls make noises to **communicate**. They hoot, whistle, and click their beaks. Their sounds travel for miles.

Most owls sleep during the day and hunt for food at night. Snowy owls are different. They are awake during the day. They hunt in the morning and evening.

OUTSTANDING OWLS!

Snowy owls save extra food and eat snow when they are thirsty.

Looking for Food

The owl is flying low. It's hunting. The owl swoops down and grabs a **lemming**. It swallows the lemming in one gulp. Snowy owls also eat rabbits and fish.

Where Do Snowy Owls Live?

Snowy owls live in the Arctic in summer. In winter, they **migrate**. They fly long distances looking for food.

You see another snowy owl. Snowy owls usually live alone. They gather where there is lots of food. A group of snowy owls is called a **blizzard**.

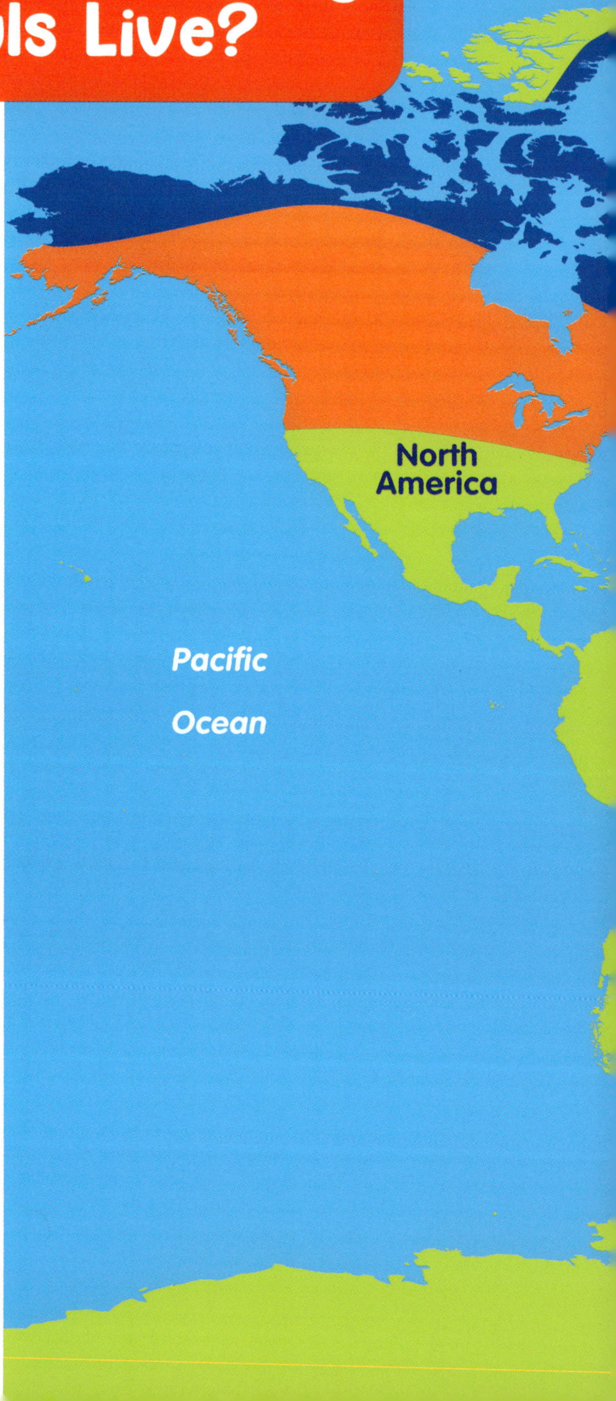

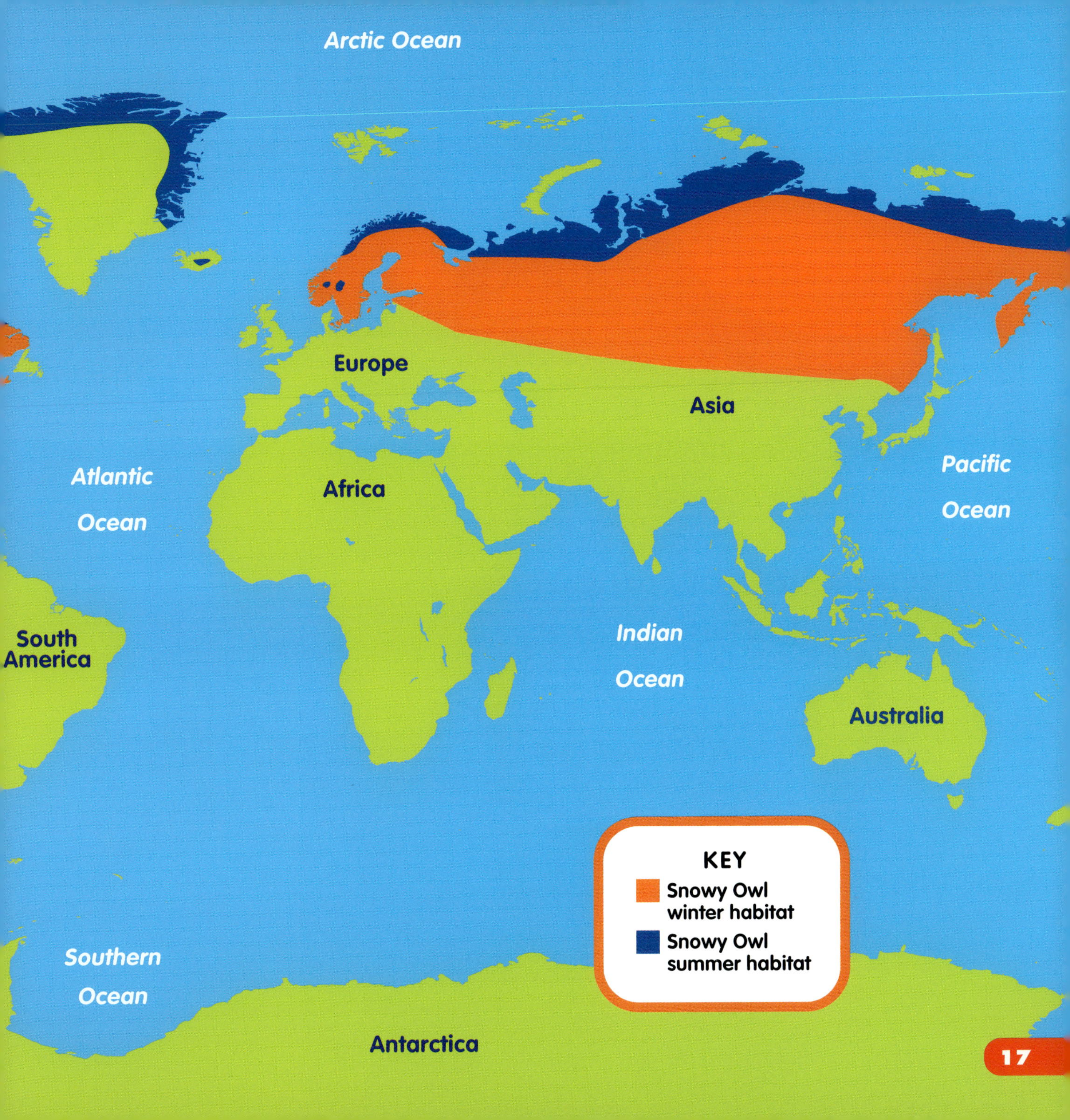
Arctic Ocean
Europe
Asia
Atlantic
Ocean
Africa
Pacific
Ocean
South
America
Indian
Ocean
Australia
Southern
Ocean
Antarctica
KEY
Snowy Owl
winter habitat
Snowy Owl
summer habitat

OUTSTANDING OWLS!

Snowy owls build their nests on the ground.

Snowy Owl Families and the Future

You see babies in a nest! Baby owls are called **owlets**. They hatch from eggs. Owlets are the size of a small apple. They have soft feathers.

Snowy owls can live for 10 years. **Pollution** harms them. Maybe someday you will see a snowy owl.

Parts of a Snowy Owl

Ears

Snowy owls have small ear holes on the sides of their heads. Their hearing is so good that they can hear small animals under the snow.

Eyes

Snowy owls have amazing vision. They can spot a lemming from over 300 feet away—the length of a football field.

Beak

Birds have hard, pointed mouths called beaks. Snowy owls have sharp, strong beaks. They use their beaks to eat and clean their feathers.

Feathers

Snowy owls are covered head to toe with thick feathers. Their feathers keep them warm and help them fly. Owls fly silently because the ends of their feathers are soft.

Talons

Talons are claws shaped like hooks. Snowy owls have sharp, powerful, black talons to catch and squeeze their food.

Glossary

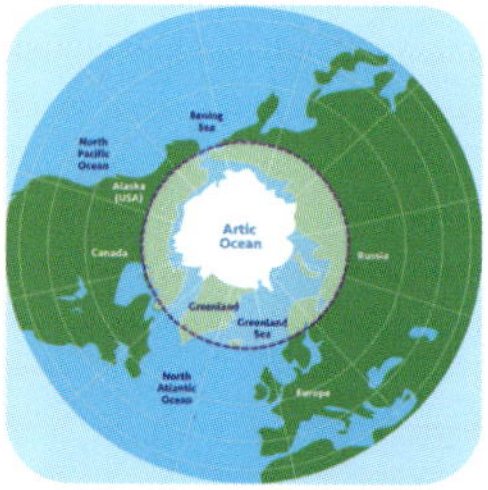

arctic (ARK-tik) a very cold place near the top of the Earth where there is lots of ice and snow

blizzard (bliz-erd) a group of snowy owls. A snow storm is also called a blizzard

communicate (kuh-myoon-i-kayt) to share ideas or feelings by making sounds or movements

lemming (lem-ing) a small mouse-like animal

migrate (my-grate) to travel in search of food or better weather

owlet (ow-let) a baby owl

pollution (poh-lew-shun) dirty air, land, and water

Quiz

1. Do Snowy Owls live underground?

A. Yes B. No

2. Do Snowy Owls have warm feathers?

A. Yes B. No

3. Do Snowy Owls eat plants?

A. Yes B. No

4. Are Snowy Owl babies called owlets?

A. Yes B. No

ANSWER KEY:

1. No
2. Yes
3. No
4. Yes

Further Reading

Barnes, Rachel. *Snowy Owls.*
Bloomington, MN: Bellwether, 2024.

Geron, Eric. *Spotted Eagle-Owl or Snowy Owl?*
New York, NY: Scholastic, 2022.

Markle, Sandra. *Snowy Owl Invasion!*
Minneapolis, MN: Lerner Publishing Group, 2022.

On the Internet

Nesting Snowy Owls

https://www.owlresearchinstitute.org/owl-live-cams
Watch a video of a snowy owl with owlets.

Snowy Owls

https://kids.nationalgeographic.com/animals/birds/facts/snowy-owl
Read more and see pictures of snowy owls.

Snowy Owl Sounds

https://www.allaboutbirds.org/guide/Snowy_Owl/sounds
Listen to the sounds snowy owls make.

Index

About the Author

Kerrily Sapet has written more than 40 books for kids. She lives near Chicago with her family. Owls are some of her favorite animals. She loves seeing and hearing them on hikes and sometimes in her backyard. Sapet has never seen snowy owls in the wild. She hopes to see one someday.